Keen Teens

Volume 3

Old Folks
Max Posner

The Lost Girl, or First Chair
Lauren Yee

The Astonishing and Dangerous
History of Mazefield the Frog
Jen Silverman

A Samuel French Acting Edition

SAMUELFRENCH.COM
SAMUELFRENCH-LONDON.CO.UK

ISBN 978-0-573-70433-8

www.SamuelFrench.com

www.SamuelFrench-London.co.uk

FOR PRODUCTION ENQUIRIES

UNITED STATES AND CANADA
Info@SamuelFrench.com
1-866-598-8449

UNITED KINGDOM AND EUROPE
Plays@SamuelFrench-London.co.uk
020-7255-4302

Each title is subject to availability from Samuel French, depending upon country of performance. Please be aware that *OLD FOLKS; THE LOST GIRL, OR FIRST CHAIR;* and *THE ASTONISHING AND DANGEROUS HISTORY OF MAZEFIELD THE FROG* may not be licensed by Samuel French in your territory. Professional and amateur producers should contact the nearest Samuel French office or licensing partner to verify availability.

No one shall make any changes in these plays for the purpose of production. No part of this book may be reproduced, stored in a retrieval system, or transmitted in any form, by any means, now known or yet to be invented, including mechanical, electronic, photocopying, recording, videotaping, or otherwise, without the prior written permission of the publisher. No one shall upload these titles, or part of these titles, to any social media websites.

For all enquiries regarding motion picture, television, and other media rights, please contact Samuel French.

MUSIC USE NOTE

Licensees are solely responsible for obtaining formal written permission from copyright owners to use copyrighted music in the performance of this play and are strongly cautioned to do so. If no such permission is obtained by the licensee, then the licensee must use only original music that the licensee owns and controls. Licensees are solely responsible and liable for all music clearances and shall indemnify the copyright owners of the plays and their licensing agent(s), Samuel French, against any costs, expenses, losses and liabilities arising from the use of music by licensees. Please contact the appropriate music licensing authority in your territory for the rights to any incidental music.

IMPORTANT BILLING AND CREDIT REQUIREMENTS

If you have obtained performance rights to this title, please refer to your licensing agreement for important billing and credit requirements.

TABLE OF CONTENTS

Foreword 7

Keen Teens Angels.....................................8

Old Folks..9

The Lost Girl, or First Chair 45

The Astonishing and Dangerous History of Mazefield the Frog 83

FOREWORD

In 2007, Keen Company developed an exciting vision for how young actors could benefit from collaboration with professional playwrights and directors, and how those playwrights could be inspired to create meaningful work that would form a new canon of dramatic literature for young people. Since then, our Keen Teens program has created dozens of contemporary plays written especially for teenagers, including the great writers represented in this collection.

Each season, we welcome young actors from all five boroughs of New York City and beyond. They come down from the Bronx and Queens after school, they commute from Brooklyn and Staten Island for weekly rehearsals, and they make this commitment on top of their schoolwork, their college planning, their school plays and their busy lives.

In Max Posner's *Old Folks*, elderly characters look back on a single moment from their youth. (In a neat theatrical trick, the teenaged actors become the senior characters' avatars.) The character Jean had been a sign language interpreter for the Broadway production of *West Side Story*. Although Max and I have never spoken about it, I've always noted that the moment Jean chooses to remember involves taking the stage in a New York City theater as a young person, as the actor who plays her does the same.

Our Keen Teens alumni have gone on to influence our world both through and beyond their acting. In Lauren Yee's *The Lost Girl*, young people impacted by the power of the performing arts go on to realize rich adult lives both through and beyond their music. The same is true for our Keen Teens actors—who are inspired by the singular power of art and find success in many fields. Wherever their lives lead them, we hope that, like Jean, they'll always remember that time they took the stage on 42nd Street.

On behalf of Keen Company, thank you for reading and producing these new plays!

– *Mark Armstrong*
Director of New Work
Keen Company

KEEN TEENS ANGELS

Old Folks

Max Posner

OLD FOLKS was first presented by Keen Company (Jonathan Silverstein, Artistic Director; Mark Armstrong, Director of New Work) and Samuel French, Inc. as part of the 2015 Keen Teens Festival of New Work. The performance was directed by Mark Armstrong, with sets by Stephen H. Carmody, costumes by Katja Andreiev, lights by Rob Ross, and sound by Elisheba Ittoop. The Production Manager was Peter Smith and the Stage manager was Sean McCain. The cast was as follows:

FRANNY	Ella Campos
TINA	Romy Bavli
SANDY	Maria Broom
HAROLD	Yordy Rosso
RON	Steve Alvarez
STEVE	Devante Rowe
GREG	Craig Steeley
JEAN	Francesca Iannacone
BETTY	Jessy Jogodnik
SAM	Hillel Rosenshine

CHARACTERS

FRANNY

TINA

SANDY

HAROLD

RON

STEVE

GREG

JEAN

BETTY

SAM

They are all elderly.

They should all be played by teenagers.

They shouldn't be made to look old.

SETTING

A nursing home in America. 2015.

ONE

(Ten people in an old folks home. Very dim lighting. We shouldn't be able to see much of anyone, maybe they are facing away from us, in wheelchairs.)

HAROLD. Martha died.

FRANNY. Sweet Martha.

RON. Sensitive Martha.

SANDY. Poor Martha.

STEVE. Poof.

JEAN. Boom.

BETTY. Dead.

GREG. How old?

HAROLD. Ninety-two.

FRANNY. I thought ninety-one.

STEVE. No, ninety-seven.

TINA. Nothing special.

JEAN. She died of old age.

STEVE. Nothing terrible.

BETTY. Nothing special.

HAROLD. We had a good time. Martha and I.

STEVE. Well we had a wild time. Martha and I.

RON. We had a terrible time.

HAROLD. We had three children.

FRANNY. We had dinner three times.

BETTY. I babysat her niece once.

RON. I walked her home twice.

GREG. Martha who?

BETTY. We wrote each other letters.

HAROLD. We wrote each other emails.

JEAN. I saw her at the doctor's recently.

HAROLD. I wrote her a text I don't know if she got it.

JEAN. At least I think it was her.

HAROLD. I wonder if anyone ever gets my texts.

BETTY. All her letters burned in a fire if I remember.

JEAN. I was getting my hip replaced.

HAROLD. She was always late.

RON. We had some screaming matches.

STEVE. We never fought.

HAROLD. She never forgave me.

GREG. She never remembered me.

FRANNY. We were in love with the same man for seven months. Sam.

HAROLD. She wasn't in love with Sam.

FRANNY. Yes she was.

SAM. I'm right here guys.

HAROLD. She HATED Sam.

SAM. I'm right here Harold.

HAROLD. She couldn't even remember Sam's name.

SAM. I'm right here.
    And that's not true.

HAROLD. Also, Sam. Your vacuum cleaner is so loud I can't sleep. You're always vacuuming.

GREG. He's right Sam.

TINA. *That's* what that sound is.

SAM. It was a long time ago.

BETTY. You can say that again.

TINA. She wouldn't recognize me like this.

SANDY. It was a long time ago.

GREG.	FRANNY.
Eisenhower was president.	Truman was president.
	Harry S. Truman.

JEAN. We tried Thai food together.

BETTY. We were enemies on a camping trip for seven days.

SAM. She said she tried Thai food for the first time with *me*.

TINA. We had the same nurse for six months.

SANDY. She was The Nurse to my Juliet in 1945.

RON. She had a little dog? Daisy?

HAROLD. I think so yes I think so.

TINA. We had the same therapist too.

HAROLD. Daisy is still living.

GREG. I remember Daisy more than Martha.

SANDY. The day the war ended she forgot all her lines.

GREG. Maybe I'll rescue Daisy.

TINA. She'd always be weeping waiting for the elevator after her session. We waved at each other. Barely. With our pinkies.

RON. We tried to rescue each other but that was naïve.

SANDY. I never forgave her. I forgot about that.

HAROLD. We went out to dinner the night our divorce went through.

TINA. When our therapist died we didn't see each other much.

HAROLD. She always interrupted me mid-sentence.

SANDY. She never said much.

BETTY. She was too polite in those days.

RON. She had green hair in those days.

SAM. She talked about you. Pillows everywhere. Talking about you.

JEAN. She dyed her hair brown but we all knew it was white.

TINA. When her husband died she got another husband and when he died she got a boyfriend, she had her pick of the old guys she always had her pick.

BETTY. So few men our age.

SAM. I was sure I'd go first.

BETTY. If you are a woman and you're sitting next to man your same age there's an eighty percent chance you will outlive him.

HAROLD. Her funeral is starting now.

SAM. I can't make it.

RON. I can't move.

JEAN. I can't take another funeral.

STEVE. It's supposed to snow later.

RON. I thought it was tomorrow.

STEVE. It's supposed to snow.

GREG. I barely knew her.

JEAN. I don't want to show up looking like this.

BETTY. I have a Skype call.

FRANNY. I don't go to churches.

SANDY. I don't like open caskets.

STEVE. Harvey was going to drive me.

SANDY. I can't drive these days.

STEVE. Harvey overslept.
He's still sleeping.

SAM. I cannot bear to see her face injected with color and chemicals. I cannot bear to see which one of us will be sadder.

HAROLD. Yes I can't bear to see her eyebrows taped on her dead hands drowning in arthritis.

SAM. And they said it would cost us sixty dollars to get a ride from our retirement home

HAROLD. You know what I could do with Sixty Dollars?

SAM. Actually, no.

HAROLD. We decided to stay here at the nursing –

SAM. Retirement –

JEAN. At our home.

TINA. And remember her. Her young little face. With you.

TWO

(Bright light on **SAM**. *He looks like a teenager. He speaks like a teenager.)*

SAM. This is what I used to look like.

This is how I used to sound.

When I asked her to the prom I looked a lot like this.

I got down on my knee.

This is how that looked.

(He gets down on one knee.)

She said no, she already had a date.

When we were eating the Thai food

My hands looked like this.

This is how she remembered them.

I used to sing a lot.

I had a bad voice.

That was part of the appeal.

I'd sing little songs very privately.

This is how they used to sound.

Actually.

I don't feel comfortable singing in front of people.

But this is how my face and body looked in those days.

Martha had a short temper.

I was this tall back then.

We never lived together.

She lived with Harold for a couple decades.

We lost touch.

I saw her with her green hair once leaving the DMV.

I wonder if it said HAIR: GREEN on her driver's license.

I used to look like this when I drove a station wagon when I got my license.

I taught her to drive stick shift.

We went our separate ways.

I used to be very messy.
Back when I looked like this.
Now I'm a neat freak.
I lint brush everything.
I vacuum all night long.
It makes me really happy.

THREE

(In the nursing home, low lighting.)

BETTY. Sam died.

GREG. When?

BETTY. Ten minutes ago.

HAROLD. No more vacuuming!

FRANNY. Harold.

HAROLD. He lived a good life.

STEVE. He was good at soccer.

JEAN. I went to his Bar Mitzvah!

SANDY. We always disagreed in book club.

GREG. Who was Sam?

SANDY. You know Sam, Greg.

TINA. He was your friend!

STEVE. Your best friend!

GREG. I don't believe in best friends.

BETTY. What?

GREG. I don't believe in best friends.

I don't like hierarchies.

TINA. I've had forty best friends.

JEAN. At least.

FRANNY. You're my best friend, Jean.

HAROLD. I cut the cord off his vacuum cleaner last night.

BETTY. What?

HAROLD. I went in while he was sleeping.

He never locks the door.

I went in with a scissors and I cut the cord off his vacuum cleaner.

So that we wouldn't have to hear it anymore.

SANDY. And now he's dead.

HAROLD. I feel so guilty.

SANDY. I knew him when he had acne and braces and crushes on everyone.

TINA. When's the funeral?

BETTY. Tomorrow.

JEAN. Supposed to snow.

STEVE. My daughter's coming to visit.

BETTY. I have to Skype.

JEAN. I didn't know Sam very well.

HAROLD. Sam knew Martha.

FRANNY. What time tomorrow?

TINA. Afternoon.

   I'll be there.

GREG. I'm having a surgery.

HAROLD. I'll be there.

STEVE. It's at a Temple?

SANDY. It's gonna cost sixty dollars to get there.

TINA. I can't afford that.

HAROLD. I'll be there.

FOUR

*(**TINA** in bright light.)*

TINA. This is how I used to sound.

This is how my face looked.

We were playing the first ever game of spin-the-bottle.

The first recorded game of spin-the-bottle.

And on the first bottle spin,

I had to kiss Sam.

Sam had to kiss me.

We were very worried that Solomon's parents were going to come downstairs and catch us. We were very worried that we would not be able to do this.

We laughed a lot.

Nervous laughter.

We went to separate colleges.

I had two daughters.

They played spin the bottle in my basement.

Then they started spinning little bottles on their iPads.

On the App.

On the Spin the Bottle iPad App.

One time I caught them in the basement.

All these boys and girls after a birthday party playing with the App.

I got mad at them.

I told them they were being inappropriate and I would tell all their parents.

And I suddenly remembered Sam. Laughing nervously into my face.

And then

Years later

Here we were.

Sam and Tina.

Just like middle school except we couldn't really get around.

But whenever I saw him he looked sixteen.
And I felt sixteen.
And I laughed nervously.
And we ate breakfast.
And I went to my room.
And he went to his room.
And he vacuumed.
And one time he saw my daughter and he said
"She looks just like you, Tina".

FIVE

(The home, dim.)

RON. Tina died.

STEVE. Lovely Tina.

HAROLD. She was the most considerate.

FRANNY. She was the most competitive.

GREG. She was the most mysterious.

JEAN. I never got to know her.

RON. We had a really nice chat last week.

GREG. Who's Tina?

SANDY. She lived a long one.

STEVE. She always complained about breakfast.

BETTY. Our Bat Mitzvahs were on the same day.

RON. I went to hers.

BETTY. Everyone went to hers.

SIX

(**BETTY** *in bright light.*)

BETTY. I didn't want to have a Bat Mitzvah.
But my mom said I would make history.
Since no girls had Bat Mitzvahs back then
And I wanted to make history
You'll make history, Betty.
And so I said SURE, I'll do it.
I looked exactly like this that day.
I invited the whole class.
A few weeks before I got an invitation to Tina's.
Same exact time.
Same exact day.
She wanted to make history too, I suppose.
I almost canceled mine but my mother wouldn't let me.
I was so nervous my stomach wouldn't stop growling.
I couldn't sleep.
I learned how to pronounce all the words in Hebrew but
I didn't learn what they meant
I was excited to sing in front of my entire class
But no one came
I saw the pictures of everyone dancing at Tina's
I saw the pictures of Tina getting lifted in a chair
I saw the boys all wearing ties and suits for the first time ever
I saw the pictures of mine
Looking like this
Surrounded by old people and cousins
No young people who weren't blood relatives
They were all at Tina's
They were watching Tina make history.
I wondered if I had made history

I realized I probably hadn't
Every year I would have the same nightmare
It was my Bat Mitzvah
And I didn't remember how to say anything
And no one was there
And I wasn't wearing a dress
And my hair was a mess
And I was late
I had that dream last night.

SEVEN

(The home, night, dimly lit.)

FRANNY. Betty died.

SANDY. Poor Betty.

FRANNY. She never got my jokes.

SANDY. She always talked about her dreams.

STEVE. Nothing as boring as other people's dreams.

GREG. I don't remember her dreams at all.

RON. She hit my car once.

Accidentally.

She was very nice about it.

She gave me her insurance information right away.

JEAN. She wasn't very nice to other women.

SANDY. She was nice to me.

JEAN. I guess she wasn't threatened by you.

FRANNY. She never remembered who I was.

Even though I went to her Bat Mitzvah.

JEAN. That wasn't hers.

That was Tina's.

FRANNY. I swear it was hers.

JEAN. That was Tina's.

SANDY. What difference does it make.

HAROLD. She's not having a funeral.

GREG. She's having a memorial service.

JEAN. What's the difference.

FRANNY. I'm not exactly sure.

SANDY. My kids and Tina's kids used to get into trouble together.

I think they broke into a swimming pool once.

I think the principal was always calling both of us in for conferences.

STEVE. I was a principal for two years.

GREG. She was always watching princess movies in the corner.

JEAN. I was like
Are you ninety or are you nine??

HAROLD. She was a good person.

SANDY. She was a good person.

GREG. She was a great person.

EIGHT

*(**RON** in the light.)*

RON. I went to a protest once.

I looked like this.

We were protesting the bomb.

It was a small protest.

It was a Saturday.

I was wearing this shirt.

My face looked like this.

Tina was there.

We were shouting things in unison.

I thought "who's that?"

And then I thought, keep protesting

You are not here to meet people, Ron

You are here to change the world.

And so I never really introduced myself

And in the end they did drop the bomb and that did end the war and

After the protest I went and had a milkshake with my friend Eddie

I asked him who that was

He said her name was Tina

I said do you know how to get in touch with her

He said no

I said do you know anyone who knows how to get in touch with her

He said no

I said

That's too bad

Ten years later I met a different woman also named Tina and we spent our entire lives together.

We had a lot of fun.

She was a morning person.

I was a night person.

So we mainly communicated in the afternoon.
We had a couple kids.
They're great.
They visit.
They look just like me.
They go to protests.
They send me pictures.
I showed them to Tina.
She said "nice looking kids"
I said "thanks"

NINE

(The home, dark.)

FRANNY. Ron died.

GREG. What an interesting man.

STEVE. He didn't have a sense of humor.

FRANNY. His children were very attractive.

SANDY. He missed his wife, you could tell.

JEAN. You could tell he was a very interesting young man back in the day.

STEVE. He spoke so loudly.

HAROLD. You're thinking of Don.

We're talking about Ron.

STEVE. I was thinking of Don too.

GREG. Who's Ron?

HAROLD. He kept to himself.

SANDY. He slept with his lights on.

FRANNY. I knew him in school he always looked tired he was obsessed with lions.

JEAN. The funeral is TBA.

HAROLD. What's TBA?

GREG. To Be Announced.

STEVE. I'd like to go.

JEAN. It'd be good to get out.

TEN

*(**STEVE** in the light)*

STEVE. I was the president of our student council.

I was the editor of our yearbook.

I was the worst player on the football team.

I broke my wrist three times in one year.

I had the whole school sign my cast.

I looked like this.

This is what I used to look like.

But I had a cast on.

With lots of signatures.

I would read them at night as I fell asleep.

I liked having people sign my cast.

I think that's why I kept breaking my wrist.

I was really into pranks.

In fact, two of the times I broke my wrists were pranks.

I didn't really break it.

I just convinced the doctor I had so that he would put a cast on me.

One time I broke my leg,

As a prank.

And that cast was very big.

And people signed my leg.

But I couldn't read them as easily.

Last week I was feeling bored and low.

So I had Ron fold me into Harold's fold-out bed when he was at the doctor's.

And Harold's daughter came to visit.

And he unfolded the couch.

And there I was.

And they were so frightened!

I couldn't stop laughing.

But they didn't laugh.

They called security.
Security didn't get the joke.
I told them I was a prankster.
I told them how I filled our high school with mice one morning.
How I covered doorknobs with Vaseline.
They gave me a warning.
Whatever that means.

ELEVEN

(The home, dim light.)

GREG. Steve cracked me up.

HAROLD. Steve freaked me out.

SANDY. I thought the couch thing was so funny!

FRANNY. He was always pretending he was sick.

GREG. He *was* sick.

JEAN. He was not sick.

HAROLD. He died in his sleep.

GREG. He died of old age.

FRANNY. He was lucky.

HAROLD. I wish I had been nicer to him.

SANDY. You weren't mean to him.

HAROLD. But I could have been nicer.

JEAN. *C'est la vie.*

FRANNY. Speak English.

TWELVE

(**JEAN** *in the light.*)

JEAN. I used to know sign language.

I used to look like this.

And I would translate musicals into sign language

For the deaf people

When I was in high school

That was my job

So when *West Side Story* came out

I was the one turning it into sign language

Standing in front of the stage

I can sing the whole show in sign language

But it made me sad that those people wouldn't get to hear how it sounded

You know?

The music was so good

Great tunes

I wore a very nice outfit to the show always.

I got lots of compliments.

And Steve actually saw the show once.

He saw the show while I was doing the sign language.

He looked so young and I looked like this

And

He recognized me!

When he moved into Elmwood he recognized me!

He said I was distracting from the musical

He said he kept missing out on the dancing because he was watching my hands

I think he was flirting with me.

I think he wanted a little company in these last years.

I tried to flirt back but I don't think I did a very good job.

He asked me if I remembered sign language.

I don't.
But he said I looked the same.
Wasn't that nice?
I looked the same.

THIRTEEN

(The home, night.)

SANDY. Jean died.

GREG. She was hard to get to know.

FRANNY. She was my best friend.

GREG. Am I thinking of the right person?

HAROLD. But did you know her?

SANDY. She didn't really.

FRANNY. Yes I did!

SANDY. It's hard meeting people when you're in your eighties.

Especially if you don't know what they used to look like.

What they used to be like.

GREG. I think you can always tell.

SANDY. Really?

GREG. Yeah.

This place is like high school.

FRANNY. No it's not.

GREG. Everyone talking behind each other's backs!

Everyone flirting!

Everyone unsure what to do!

SANDY. Oh I don't think so Greg.

HAROLD. Greg you never remember anyone.

GREG. I know.

FRANNY. It's not his fault.

SANDY. It's frustrating.

GREG. I'm bad with names.

I know everyone's face.

But once they're gone and it's just a name…

HAROLD. I saw photos from Martha's funeral.

SANDY. Oh?

HAROLD. Our kids emailed them to me.

I saw videos.

FRANNY. And?

HAROLD. It was really nice.

FOURTEEN

(GREG in the light)

GREG. This is how I used to look before I went fully bald.

When I was an encyclopedia.

That's what they called me.

The Encyclopedia.

I studied art history.

So I was always memorizing the names of different painters.

Different artists and years and countries and paintings.

I could keep track of all of them.

I was basically a computer.

My kids used to make fun of me.

We'd go to museums and I would be very competitive.

I would try to guess every single artwork.

And my son Jeremy would say

DAD, CAN YOU JUST ENJOY THE ART?

And I'd say, I AM ENJOYING THE ART

Jeremy came to visit last week and everyone said

You look just like Greg but with hair

He looked just like this

He hates memorizing things

He doesn't know which state is which on a map

He doesn't know who painted what

He doesn't know who is the president of which country

And I'm like

JEREMY. YOU SHOULD MEMORIZE THAT STUFF

But he won't

And I don't really remember all of it anymore

If I SEE the painting I know who made it

But if I just hear the name, I can't picture it

Anyways

My voice used to sound like this

It's a nice sound, isn't it?

FIFTEEN

(The home.)

SANDY. Poor Greg.

HAROLD. He couldn't remember anything.

FRANNY. He could remember you.

HAROLD. How could anyone forget me??

SANDY. I forget you every night and every morning I'm like. OH NO. It's Harold.

HAROLD. Hey.

FRANNY. She's just joking.

HAROLD. I thought his funeral was tomorrow.

SANDY. It was yesterday.

I went.

FRANNY. How was it?

SANDY. It was slow.

But good.

Lots of photos of him as a kid.

Good looking kid.

Lots of hair on his head.

FRANNY. I told you to wake me up.

I wanted to go.

SANDY. I'll take you to the next one.

FRANNY. Promise?

SANDY. I promise.

HAROLD. I want to come too.

SIXTEEN

(**FRANNY** *in the light.*)

FRANNY. I was a cheerleader.

Are there still cheerleaders?

This is how I used to look.

I would yell GO LIONS very loudly.

It was an act of rebellion.

My family thought all cheerleaders were dumb.

They thought high schoolers should spend their time reading books and doing plays.

So I didn't read books and I didn't do plays and I tried out for cheerleading.

They threw me into the air and they caught me.

My fellow cheerleders.

It's a sport, you know?

It takes a lot of athleticism.

Greg said he saw me cheer.

He went to one of the games?

He memorized all the football players.

He made little sports cards for them.

For the high school.

Made them all feel important.

He remembered because that was the game where they dropped me.

Michelle dropped me on purpose.

She was very mean.

You know about mean girls?

How girls can be especially mean when they're fifteen?

Well that was true in the 1930s, that was true in the 1950s, that was true in the 1980s, it's true now and it will definitely be true in a hundred years.

But later on we forgave each other.

I saw Michelle picking her kids up from school.

And she saw me.

And we both looked like teenagers
We were young mothers
And she said I'm so sorry Franny.
And it meant the world to me.
She had been losing sleep over it for years.
People regret being mean I've found.
I was mean.
I was a mean girl.
As an experiment.
For a few years.
And I tracked down every person I remembered being
mean to.
On Facebook I tracked them down.
And I wrote them long letters.
And they each replied.
And some of them didn't remember.
I showed them how I looked in high school.
I looked like this.
And then they all remembered.
And that made me feel really good.

SEVENTEEN

(The home, low light.)

HAROLD. That was a very full funeral.

SANDY. Jean was so nice to everyone.

HAROLD. She was.

SANDY. I don't like this place without her.

HAROLD. You don't like me.

SANDY. You're just another old man, Harold.

HAROLD. I know.

SANDY. How did you used to look?

HAROLD. I don't remember.

How did you used to look?

SANDY. I'm not really sure.

I wish I could show you.

HAROLD. If I stare at you, I think I can see.

(lighting shift, from dim to bright)

Yes!

SANDY. You have a full head of hair!

HAROLD. You don't have any wrinkles.

SANDY. You're three inches taller.

HAROLD. Your hair is bright red.

SANDY. You look like

Hal

From my high school!

HAROLD. I went by Hal in high school.

SANDY. You're Hal!

HAROLD. Yes.

You're…

SANDY. Sandy!

Remember?

Oh my god.

We did a play together?

And we fought each other in Debate?

Brutally?

HAROLD. Yes!

SANDY. You were Antony!

HAROLD. And you were Cleopatra!

SANDY. You look the same!

HAROLD. You look the same.

SANDY. You suddenly look the same!

HAROLD. I can't believe it took us this long to recognize –

SANDY. In the debate

You argued that zoos were immoral and should be closed.

HAROLD. You argued that zoos were educational and should remain.

SANDY. Who won that debate?

HAROLD. I don't remember.

SANDY. Well.

Are there still zoos?

HAROLD. Yes.

There are.

I suppose you won.

SANDY. I suppose I did.

(lights)

End of Play

The Lost Girl, Or First Chair

Lauren Yee

THE LOST GIRL, OR FIRST CHAIR was first presented by Keen Company (Jonathan Silverstein, Artistic Director; Mark Armstrong, Director of New Work) and Samuel French, Inc. as part of the 2015 Keen Teens Festival of New Work. The performance was directed by Liz Carlson, with sets by, costumes by Katja Andreiev, lights by Rob Ross, sound by Elisheba Ittoop. The Production Manager was Peter Smith and the Stage manager was Sean McCain. The cast was as follows:

THE LOST GIRL (KATIE)	Lucille Vasquez
ROSIN	Cory Sierra
JESSICA	Elsie Razo
MESSICA	Karla Ynfante
JULIE	Liv Reis
REED	Nicholas Johnson
THE CUSTODIAN	Bahsil Moody
MRS. JACKSON	Chelsea Allison
MR. JACKSON	Hillel Rosenshine
MR. LEE	Kaisheem Fowler-Bryant
WOMAN (OR MAN) IN A BOAT	Chelsea Allison

CHARACTERS

THE LOST GIRL (KATIE) – former first chair violin, missing

ROSIN – second chair violin, perfectionist, suckup

JESSICA – third chair violin, the alpha twin

MESSICA – fourth chair violin, the beta twin

JULIE – the fifth chair violin, Katie's best friend, nondescript

REED – Julie's only other best friend, a clarinet

THE CUSTODIAN – a prophet, maybe former violin prodigy, from a nebulous eastern European country that was once ruled by a dictator

MRS. JACKSON – Julie's mother

MR. JACKSON – Julie's father

MR. LEE – former student now turned high school orchestra conductor

WOMAN (OR MAN) IN A BOAT – can be doubled with any other role

And everyone is part of the **CHORUS** when they're not playing an active role on stage

NOTES

As much action possible is contained in the slightly subterranean world of the orchestra room, which also shares the space with the marching band, the choir, and the jazz ensemble. This is a large public magnet school. A ruthless place for gifted young people. The students don't ever play music from their instruments in the course of the play, but I'm thinking maybe orchestral music punctuates scenes via sound design.

Also, with a little tweaking, any of the characters can be played by an actor of any gender.

For music underscoring that appears throughout the play, the publisher recommends that licensees create original compositions.

Scene
Music room

*(**MR. LEE** gives a tour to prospective freshmen.)*

MR. LEE. Welcome to San Leandro High's advanced orchestra, one of the district's most prestigious orchestral programs. Here are some things you should know about the orchestra:

We have fifty-two members in the advanced orchestra.

Twenty-eight of them are seniors.

Fifteen of them are juniors.

Seven of them are sophomores.

And two of them are freshmen.

Forty-seven of them are virgins.

Ten of them are addicted to painkillers.

Twenty-seven of them are incurably lonely.

Fourteen of them believe in true love.

And all fifty-two are crazy.

Which is to be expected because all orchestras every place everywhere are filled with lonely, crazy people who want to be loved, who want to love, but don't know how to do it.

I should know!

I was once a student here myself. And now I'm here.

Surprise!

But that's okay!

Because every so often, there is that sound

(music)

From that one student

(music)

That makes the whole lot of them worth it.

(The sound of violin. He closes his eyes, listens. It is beautiful. Lights up on **THE LOST GIRL**. *She looks at* **MR. LEE**, *then she disappears with the sound of the ocean.)*

Scene
Music room

(**MR. LEE** *posts a notice.*)

MR. LEE. First chair violin auditions this Friday after school. Sign up for slots. Note: This position is a TEMPORARY position. She WILL come back.

(**MR. LEE** *and some of the* **CHORUS** *exit. Lights up on the violins –* **JULIE, JESSICA, MESSICA** *– and* **REED**, *a clarinet, in a circle after practice. Maybe they're possibly a little stoned.*)

JESSICA. That is so not true. She's never coming back.

ROSIN. How do you know?

JULIE. Mr. Lee said –

JESSICA. He only said that because he's totally

MESSICA. – definitely –

JESSICA. Absolutely in love with her.

JULIE. Ew.

ROSIN. Oh, come on.

REED. You really think so?

JESSICA. He's holding auditions? C'mon, he knows who he wants. He's heard us play. He knows what we're capable of. He knows which one of us is the best.

(**MESSICA** *clears her throat.*)

Well, second best anyway. He's just delaying the inevitable. He's just stalling with this audition crap because he thinks she's gonna make it back.

ROSIN. That's crazy.

JESSICA. He keeps looking at her chair like it's gonna make her come back. It's weird.

MESSICA. I hope you'd look at my chair like that if I weirdly disappeared coming back from summer break.

JESSICA. You're my twin, not my music teacher. And if you weirdly disappeared, wouldn't I ALSO weirdly disappear?

MESSICA. True.

JULIE. She didn't weirdly disappear.

MESSICA. How do you know?

JESSICA. How DO you know?

REED. So who's it gonna be?

JULIE. What?

REED. You're the violins. This is it. So. As a humble clarinet, can I ask: who's it gonna be?

ROSIN. I think it's too early to talk about this.

JULIE. I mean, he said it was a temporary position. So if she comes back –

JESSICA. If she EVER comes back.

MESSICA. If anyone ever hears from her again.

JESSICA. This is senior year, Jackson. This is it. Sophomore year, junior year: maybe. But senior year? No one just LEAVES before senior year.

MESSICA. OR she got picked up by Juilliard.

ROSIN. People don't get "picked up by Juilliard."

MESSICA. Mr. Lee said "We are a feeder school." The San Leandro High School orchestra is basically a feeder school to Juilliard. He said –

ROSIN. I would really be surprised if someone with Katie Johnson's technique would –

MESSICA. He SAID –

ROSIN. Based on what? One person? ONE girl got picked up by Juilliard, like, fifteen years ago.

MESSICA. She WAS the best violinist this school's ever had.

JESSICA. Apparently Mr. Lee was the best violinist this school's ever had. And look where he is now.

ROSIN. And the Juilliard girl went AFTER she graduated. Not before. Not DURING her senior year, but after.

REED. Katie was really good, though.

JULIE. She IS really good.

JESSICA. Was, is.

JULIE. You talk about her like she's dead.

JESSICA. Maybe she is, Julie. I mean, no offense to you, but maybe she is.

REED. Shut up, Jessica.

JESSICA. Or she might as well be! At the very least, I feel like Mr. Lee has her in his basement or something. I mean, he NEVER takes us over to his house.

ROSIN. What teacher takes their students over to their house?

JESSICA. Mr. Schmidt? Ms. Blinick?

JULIE. Those're social studies teachers, that's not the same.

JESSICA. But we're his whole life. Most teachers have other things in their lives, like wives or kids. He doesn't have anything. He just has us. We're it.

REED. Well, that settles that!

MESSICA. Wait, so is she pregnant or is she dead?

REED. She moved. It's so obvious, right? Katie just moved and switched schools... Right?

(Everyone kind of shrugs.)

JESSICA. Okay, this is ridiculous.

JULIE. Thank you, Jessica.

JESSICA. Julie, just tell us.

JULIE. What?

JESSICA. You guys were friends.

MESSICA. BEST friends.

JULIE. No, we weren't.

JESSICA. Seemed like it.

JULIE. *(shrugs)* We were orchestra friends.

REED. Guys, if she doesn't want to talk about it –

JESSICA. So what ACTUALLY happened to her?

JULIE. Reed, it's not that I don't want to talk about it. It's just...we were just orchestra friends, okay? I don't know where she is! I don't know what happened to her, okay?

(JULIE *runs off.)*

REED. Not cool, guys.

JESSICA. I can't help it if your girlfriend is not first chair material.

REED. She's not my girlfriend.

ROSIN. Forget this. I need to practice.

JESSICA. Practice? Oh come on, Rosin, we all know you're going to be first chair.

MESSICA. Obviously.

JESSICA. You were second, and now you're going to be first. He'll just bump us all up.

ROSIN. Shut up.

MESSICA. Easy peasy.

JESSICA. Unless –

MESSICA. Unless –

ROSIN. Stop talking. Stop talking! You're going to jinx it.

JESSICA. How? / How am I gonna jinx it?

ROSIN. You're going to jinx it! You just are!

JESSICA. Whoa. Rosin. I'm just saying: "You're the most talented one here. You're obviously going to get it – "

MESSICA. " – as long as you don't screw it up."

> (**ROSIN** *storms off with her violin.*)

REED. You're making her nuts.

JESSICA. Rosin is always nuts.

MESSICA. It's just 'cause she went to private school.

REED. Though maybe she was on that plane.

MESSICA. What plane?

REED. The plane that went missing. They still haven't found it.

MESSICA. It was going from Borneo to Tokyo.

JESSICA. We would've definitely heard about it if she'd been on the missing plane.

REED. ...or not.

> (*They all muse on this.*)

But the real question is –

JESSICA & MESSICA. What?

REED. So which one of you's gonna be first chair?

Scene
By the lockers

(*JULIE closes her locker. The* CUSTODIAN, *vaguely eastern European and with a slight limp, comes up to her. The* CUSTODIAN *holds a violin case.*)

CUSTODIAN. This. Is for you.

JULIE. This isn't mine.

CUSTODIAN. This is a violin. You play the violin. You are the girl who plays the violin. The chair?

JULIE. I play violin, yes, but I'm not THE chair, I'm the fifth chair. It's not mine.

(*The* CUSTODIAN *hands the violin case to* JULIE.)

CUSTODIAN. She said it was for you. You are to have it.

JULIE. What? Who?

(*The* CUSTODIAN *limps off.*)

Wait, wait!

(REED *appears.*)

REED. Whoa, sweet new case.

JULIE. It's not mine.

REED. Then whose is it?

JULIE. I think it might be Katie's.

Scene

(**JULIE** *puts her ear to the violin case. The sound of waves, sea birds, paradise. She loses herself in the sound.* **THE LOST GIRL** – **KATIE** – *appears.*)

THE LOST GIRL. To whomever receives this message.

My name is Katie Johnson

And I am currently on an island somewhere in the middle of the Pacific Ocean

After spending three days adrift at sea.

So far, life here has been okay.

I don't have to worry about being late to fourth period

Or beating the bell to homeroom.

Here I tell time based on the sun and the tides and eat my meals according to the sound of the birds.

Oh yes, here there are birds

Beautiful ones

Not just the pigeons and seagulls that used to circle the yard when lunch ended

But birds of paradise

Which I guess is a sign that I am in some sort of paradise

And not only birds but insects

Monkeys

Lizards.

I found my phone the other day

I put it in the sand to dry it out,

But I don't have a charger, so I'm not sure what I'll do if I get it working again.

I think there might be someone else on this island.

A human

Male

Though I'm not sure.

In my mind, I named him Sven.

The island is large enough for two people so we haven't met yet.

But maybe when we do, they'll also have an iPhone 6
charger
And maybe I can call home.

Scene
Music room

*(The **CUSTODIAN** wipes down the room. Maybe the floors, maybe the tables, something like that.)*

CUSTODIAN. You will soon be done?

MESSICA. We're just sitting here.

CUSTODIAN. I have to clean up. You will go soon?

JESSICA. Mr. Lee said we could be here after school.

CUSTODIAN. I have to clean.

JESSICA. Well, we have to be here.

*(The **CUSTODIAN** grumbles, walks off.)*

MESSICA. She's so weird.

JESSICA. All Germans are weird.

*(Maybe the **CUSTODIAN** speaks with an accent or maybe she speaks in her perfect, unaccented native language.)*

CUSTODIAN. When I left my country, they took my violin. They took it from me and then they told me I had to leave or they would break my fingers one by one. So I left but before then, they still broke my fingers, one by one.

ROSIN. She's not German.

JESSICA. How would you know?

ROSIN. I spent a summer in Switzerland.

JESSICA. Switzerland is not in Germany.

CUSTODIAN. This happens a lot where I am from.
People say one thing and do the other.

ROSIN. You don't have to be in Germany to be German.

MESSICA. Guys, I'm pretty sure she's not German at all.

CUSTODIAN. It also happens a lot here, I have noticed.
People say one thing and do the other. "Thank you!" "You are welcome!" But you are NOT welcomed here. And no one really thanks you when they thank you.

JESSICA. What about Czech? Aren't Czech people really weird?

ROSIN. Prague is amazing in the summer.

CUSTODIAN. Growing up, I learned two things from my parents. From my father, the violin. From my mother, how to clean up other people's messes. And I always think to myself, my father was a great man, but thank god for what I learned from my mother. Otherwise, I would have nothing.

Scene

(**JULIE** *stares at the violin case.*)

REED. I think this is a sign.

JULIE. Of what?

REED. You should audition. YOU should be first chair. This was Katie's case. Soooo if she gave it to you…

JULIE. I can't even open it. It's stuck. I'm not even sure there's a violin inside.

REED. So?

JULIE. Plus, I'm fifth chair. Even if I was remotely qualified to audition, there are three people ahead of me who deserve it more than me.

REED. No, there is Rosin, who is psycho and therefore, undesirable. And then there's Jessica and Messica, who don't even count.

JULIE. Why don't they count?

REED. A. They're twins, they do everything together. And B. It's called "first chair," not "first chairs." so they can't BOTH do it.

JULIE. My freshman year, he stopped me after two notes.

REED. What?

JULIE. I got two notes in before he said to stop. That was my whole audition.

REED. First chair is not just about playing ability. It's also about a lot of other things.

JULIE. Like what?

MRS. JACKSON. Reed, are you staying for dinner?

REED. Nah, I gotta get back, Mrs. Jackson. And Julie's gotta practice.

MRS. JACKSON. For what?

JULIE. Nothing.

MRS. JACKSON. Nothing?

REED. Bye, Julie! Good luck.

(**REED** *exits.*)

MRS. JACKSON. I hear you're going to try out for first chair.

JULIE. Mom!

MRS. JACKSON. You need any help?

JULIE. NO.

MRS. JACKSON. Julie, I was in that same orchestra when I went there. I know how it works.

JULIE. I'm fifth chair!

MRS. JACKSON. You just need to demonstrate initiative.

JULIE. If I had initiative, I wouldn't be fifth chair. There wasn't even supposed to be a fifth chair.

MRS. JACKSON. But there was! And you're it!

JULIE. So I don't have initiative! I don't even know what that means!

(**MR. JACKSON** *enters.*)

MRS. JACKSON. Honey, when your father met me, did he like me?

MR. JACKSON. No!

MRS. JACKSON. Did he even find me remotely attractive?

MR. JACKSON. Not in the slightest! I never kissed a girl in my life!

MRS. JACKSON. But what did I do?

MR. JACKSON. What DID you do?

JULIE. *(heard it before)* Yeah, what DID you do?

MRS. JACKSON. I walked right up to your father, third day of class, and I said to him, I said, "I like you."

MR. JACKSON. "I like you a lot."

MRS. JACKSON. "And you're going to like me."

MR. JACKSON. "One day you're going to marry me."

MRS. JACKSON. "And until then – "

MR. JACKSON. "I will hunt you down."

MRS. JACKSON. "I will hunt you down."

MR. JACKSON. "I will hunt you down, I will salt your fields, I will sack your city, I will steal your women and I will kill your men until I make you mine."

MRS. JACKSON. Did I say that? Did I really say that?

MR. JACKSON. That's how I remember it. But this was back in seventh grade. Seventh grade: how about that for persistence, huh?

MRS. JACKSON. "Salt your fields!" I don't even think I know what that means. That was probably just something I read in school. Ha!

JULIE. I hope you don't tell other people that story. That is not a good story.

MR. JACKSON. I think it's a great story.

MRS. JACKSON. I tell it all the time. It's a story about love!

MR. JACKSON. Your mother's variety anyway.

MRS. JACKSON. But the point is –

JULIE. What IS the point, Mom?

MRS. JACKSON. The point is

MR. JACKSON. The point IS …you've got to keep trying.

MRS. JACKSON. You've got to keep trying!

MR. JACKSON. You've got to fling yourself headfirst and just say –

MRS. JACKSON. "I love you. I have always loved you, and if you don't love me back, who knows what I will do?"

MR. JACKSON. – so to speak.

MRS. JACKSON. Just audition, right? Try out. You love orchestra.

JULIE. I love BEING IN the orchestra. There's a difference.

MRS. JACKSON. "You love being in orchestra." No difference.

JULIE. I love being AROUND the orchestra. Not being first chair.

MRS. JACKSON. OR you don't want to be first chair because Katie was first chair.

JULIE. That's not what this is about at all!

MRS. JACKSON. You want me to talk to him?

JULIE. Who?

MRS. JACKSON. Mr. Lee. He went to high school with us, you know. *(to* **MR. JACKSON***)* Kevin Lee.

MR. JACKSON. Oh, Kevin! Kevin Kevlar! How is he?

MRS. JACKSON. He had a crush on me, you know.

MR. JACKSON. I didn't know this. Did you tell me this?

MRS. JACKSON. We had orchestra together. What can I say? I made the best brownies.

JULIE. Mom: Don't. It's probably already been decided anyway.

MRS. JACKSON. Well, that's not very fair. Does that sound very fair?

MR. JACKSON. Let Julie do it her way.

JULIE. Seriously.

MRS. JACKSON. All right, all right! I won't get involved.

JULIE. Thank you.

(*JULIE exits.*)

MRS. JACKSON. …that much.

Scene
On the island

THE LOST GIRL. When I was in high school, I used to think of the violin all the time.

I used to think of everything in terms of music.

Now I think about things like:

What will the weather be like?

Will it rain?

What will we eat?

How will I cook it?

Is the water safe to drink?

What color was the sky before I went to bed last night?

Simple things.

And I can't remember a time when I thought of anything else

Even though I know just a short while ago, my mind was full of things like backpacks and pencil cases and what college I might go to if I went to college and what kind of things I'd have to do to get into whatever college I decided I want to go to.

But here:

Eat.

Drink.

Sit.

And wait for the sky to change color.

Scene
Music room

> (JESSICA *and* MESSICA *practicing.*)

MESSICA. What would you do if I went missing? Would you cry?

JESSICA. Would YOU cry?

MESSICA. I think I would cry.

JESSICA. Then I would probably cry, too.

> (ROSIN *listens to something on her headphones, she seems to be talking to herself. She seems to be practicing some sort of intense physical violin training.*)

Look at her.

MESSICA. Look at her.

JESSICA. What is she doing?

MESSICA. What is she doing?

JESSICA. I think she's practicing.

MESSICA. Oh yeah, she's practicing.

JESSICA. THAT'S not gonna help.

MESSICA. That's SO not gonna help.

JESSICA. She's gonna choke.

MESSICA. She's gonna SO choke.

JESSICA. *(high five)* First chair!

MESSICA. *(high five)* First chair!

> (ROSIN *notices them, glares, walks off.*)

But you know we can't both be first chair, right?

JESSICA. Why not?

MESSICA. Well, there is literally ONE chair and –

JESSICA. Then we'll be first AND second chair.

MESSICA. But someone's got to be first chair and someone's got to be second.

JESSICA. We'll rotate.

MESSICA. That doesn't make sense.

JESSICA. We audition together, we get placed together.

MESSICA. …Or maybe you audition. By yourself.

JESSICA. Messica.

MESSICA. Jessica. We can't both be first chair.

JESSICA. We'll ask him. He thinks we're basically the same person. We'll ask him. And he'll have to say yes.

MESSICA. Or he'll just say no. And neither of us'll get it.

JESSICA. Then neither of us'll get it. We're the same. Not a problem.

MESSICA. Well, we're not EXACTLY the same in everything.

JESSICA. Like what?

MESSICA. Like violin. You know I'm only fourth chair 'cause you're third chair, 'cause we tried out together.

JESSICA. So?

MESSICA. Maybe I don't want to be first chair. Or second chair. Or rotate. Maybe we don't need to be together ALL the time, you know?

JESSICA. Why not?

MESSICA. Because… I'm not you. And sometimes it feels like I'm just this lesser copy of you.

JESSICA. I don't feel that about you.

MESSICA. Of course not. YOU'RE the Jessica.

JESSICA. So?

MESSICA. You're the Jessica, I'm the Messica? Messica's not even a real name.

JESSICA. Yes, it is. It's your name: It's a real name.

MESSICA. It's just a name I got named because Mom wanted something that rhymed with Jessica, okay?

JESSICA. Don't say that. You are my twin and –

MESSICA. You know people can tell us apart.

JESSICA. No, they can't.

MESSICA. We don't even look THAT much alike. We came from two completely different eggs that just happened to get fertilized at the same time. The only reason why people even remember that we're twins is because we dress alike. Most people in school think we're just weird best friends.

JESSICA. Take that back.

MESSICA. I'm sorry, but it's true.

JESSICA. Messica, you have to audition with me. I can't do this without you.

MESSICA. Well, maybe you should.

(**MESSICA** *exits.*)

JESSICA. Messica. Messica!

(**JESSICA** *runs off after her.*)

And we totally do look alike! It's not just the clothes!

Scene
Music room

(**MR. LEE** *comes out of his office.* **ROSIN** *corners him.*)

ROSIN. Mr. Lee!

MR. LEE. Ms. Martinez, it's 6:30.

ROSIN. I know.

MR. LEE. The music room's closed. Auditions are tomorrow, you realize.

ROSIN. Yes, and before then I just wanted to say – *(takes out index cards)* "What is a first chair?"

MR. LEE. Save this for tomorrow.

ROSIN. "A first chair is a leader. A first chair is a listener. A first chair is all things to all people at all times." And that can be me. I can be that. I know I can be that.

MR. LEE. Ms. Martinez, I have to get home.

ROSIN. You don't have a home.

MR. LEE. Excuse me?

ROSIN. I mean, yes, you do. You technically DO have a home, I guess, a house where you live, though none of us have ever seen it, but not in the metaphorical sense. In the metaphorical sense, you don't have a home outside of this room. Your home is here. This class is your home. This room is your home. And it's also like that for me. Mr. Lee, I could've stayed in private school. I could've gone to a conservatory program. I could've gone somewhere where I didn't have to take gym, but instead I am here. In this *(whisper)* PUBLIC SCHOOL with these PUBLIC SCHOOL HOOLIGANS. And you know why? Because of this program. Because of you. Because of this chair. So tell me what I need to do to get this. Please.

(**MRS. JACKSON** *enters with brownies.*)

MRS. JACKSON. Hi hi. Am I interrupting?

MR. LEE. Christine, what're you doing?

ROSIN. Yeah, what're you doing here?

MRS. JACKSON. Thought I'd just pop by! Drop off some brownies. You're not leaving, are you?

ROSIN. Thought you had to go home.

MR. LEE. Ms. Martinez was just leaving.

>(ROSIN *exits.*)

>(JULIE *at home with* MR. JACKSON. *Split stage.*)

JULIE. Dad, where's Mom?

MR. JACKSON. She's at work.

JULIE. Doing what?

MR. JACKSON. *(too fast)* What?!

JULIE. ...she's at work doing what?

MR. JACKSON. Nothing. Nothing. I didn't say anything. I said nothing. What did you think I was talking about?

JULIE. I...don't really know.

MR. JACKSON. What could your mother be possibly doing?!

>(MRS. JACKSON *is maybe seducing or maybe threatening* MR. LEE. *Or maybe a combination of both.*)

MRS. JACKSON. My daughter gets the chair.

MR. LEE. Christine, I'd love to, you know I would, but I'm not really sure if I can –

MRS. JACKSON. My daughter gets the chair.

MR. JACKSON. You know we'd do anything for you, right, Jules?

JULIE. Yeah?

MR. JACKSON. Just...keep that in mind, okay?

JULIE. Why?

MRS. JACKSON. Say it!

MR. JACKSON. Just...keep it in mind.

MR. LEE. She gets the chair! She gets the chair!

MRS. JACKSON. Say her name! What's her name?

MR. LEE. Julie! Julie!

MRS. JACKSON. Julie gets the chair!

MR. LEE. Julie gets the chair!

(**MR. LEE** *and* **MRS. JACKSON** *make out.*)

Scene
In the hallway

JULIE. Wait.

CUSTODIAN. Yes?

JULIE. I need to know. Did she really give this to you to give to me?

CUSTODIAN. What?

JULIE. Did she really mean for me to have this?

CUSTODIAN. Who?

JULIE. Katie.

CUSTODIAN. Yes. Katie. Katie Johnson. You forgot to clean out your locker before the summer?

JULIE. I'm not Katie.

CUSTODIAN. No?

JULIE. I'm Julie.

CUSTODIAN. Julie?

JULIE. Julie Jackson.

CUSTODIAN. That is not Katie Johnson.

JULIE. No.

CUSTODIAN. Then this is not yours.

JULIE. I guess not. I thought it was for me, though. I thought she might've given it to me. As a sign.

CUSTODIAN. She left her instrument here?

JULIE. I guess. I don't even really know if there's a violin inside.

CUSTODIAN. You have not checked?

JULIE. It doesn't open.

CUSTODIAN. For you.

JULIE. What?

CUSTODIAN. A fine case like this, it does not open for just anyone. You must know how. Here –

    (*The* **CUSTODIAN** *takes the violin case. She opens it easily.*)

JULIE. How did you do that?

CUSTODIAN. I had one just like it as a girl growing up. The hinges get stuck.

JULIE. It's empty.

CUSTODIAN. So perhaps wherever she was going, she took the violin with her.

JULIE. Perhaps.

CUSTODIAN. This friend Katie, what happened to her?

JULIE. I'm not really sure.

CUSTODIAN. You must have some idea.

Scene
On the island

THE LOST GIRL. There was a rescue boat that came by the other day. They sent out a little dinghy to come get me and the woman rowing the boat said –

WOMAN IN A BOAT. "Are you Katie Johnson? Are you The Lost Girl?"

THE LOST GIRL. And I said, "Yes, I am." And she said –

WOMAN IN A BOAT. "We've been looking for you. We rescued your parents six days ago. Please come with us."

THE LOST GIRL. And I looked at Sven, at our child, at the life that we had built together, and I smiled at the woman in the dinghy, and I said, "Thank you, but I'm fine. I think I'd like to stay."

WOMAN IN A BOAT. You sure about that?

THE LOST GIRL. Yes, I'm sure.

WOMAN IN A BOAT. It's a hard life out here. Your parents miss you.

THE LOST GIRL. I miss them, too.

WOMAN IN A BOAT. Do you have food?

THE LOST GIRL. There are fish and plants and some small animals.

WOMAN IN A BOAT. And shelter?

THE LOST GIRL. We'll be fine together.

WOMAN IN A BOAT. And what should I tell your parents?

THE LOST GIRL. Tell them that I am okay. That things are all right here. That I am happy here. I am happier than I have ever been in my whole entire life.

WOMAN IN A BOAT. They said you played the violin.

THE LOST GIRL. Yes?

WOMAN IN A BOAT. They said you were amazing.

THE LOST GIRL. Maybe.

WOMAN IN A BOAT. They said you were first chair.

THE LOST GIRL. I was.

WOMAN IN A BOAT. I would have very much liked to have heard you play.

THE LOST GIRL. Maybe in another life you would have.

WOMAN IN A BOAT. What happened?

The tide's going out.

THE LOST GIRL. You should go.

WOMAN IN A BOAT. Are you sure? I don't think we'll come back around again.

THE LOST GIRL. That's okay. I need to go feed my child and mend the roof of our hut. The rain's coming in, I can feel it.

WOMAN IN A BOAT. And what about your friend?

THE LOST GIRL. What?

WOMAN IN A BOAT. Julie. If I run into her, if she asks me, why didn't I bring you back, what should I tell her?

THE LOST GIRL. Tell her we moved. Tell her I switched schools. And for the first time in my life, I saw all these other things that people did, all these other things that I could do with my life.

JULIE. So you just gave up orchestra?

THE LOST GIRL. I wanted to try something new.

JULIE. And you gave up on me?

THE LOST GIRL. I didn't give up on you, Julie. I just… Moved, that's all.

JULIE. You never told me you were going.

THE LOST GIRL. I sent you an email.

JULIE. That's not telling.

THE LOST GIRL. I left you my violin.

JULIE. But you couldn't even give it to me yourself?

THE LOST GIRL. If you want to hang out, you know where to find me. I have cross-country after school most days now, but on the weekends, I'm usually free if we don't have a meet.

JULIE. You run cross-country?

THE LOST GIRL. I'm not that good. And I usually finish towards the back. But I like it. I like running. It's fun. It's fun in a way the violin never was.

JULIE. How could you just give it up like that? How could you just stop playing? You were FIRST CHAIR. You were our first chair.

THE LOST GIRL. I was first chair because it came easy to me. But it doesn't mean that I loved it.

JULIE. I don't believe you.

THE LOST GIRL. Up to you.

> (**THE LOST GIRL** *disappears.* **JULIE** *back in the music room.*)

Scene

(JULIE and ROSIN sit outside MR. LEE's office. Silence.)

JULIE. Why are you in the orchestra?

ROSIN. Is this a trick?

JULIE. No.

ROSIN. You're trying to distract me from the audition.

JULIE. I'm not.

ROSIN. He's gonna be out here any minute. I don't have time for this.

JULIE. I was just curious. I actually don't know the answer myself. I used to think it was because I loved music, but maybe it was just because I loved Katie and she was special. And I loved being around someone special.

ROSIN. I can't explain it. It's not language.

JULIE. Then what is it?

ROSIN. It's here. And here.

(JULIE hears the music playing in ROSIN's heart.)

JULIE. Oh. Wow.

ROSIN. That is why I'm in the orchestra.

MR. LEE. *(offstage)* Ms. Jackson?

ROSIN. Go on. Congrats.

JULIE. What do you mean?

ROSIN. Your mom and Mr. Lee. So: congrats. First chair.

JULIE. I haven't even gone in.

ROSIN. Doesn't matter. You can be first chair. All you have to do is go in there.

JULIE. I want that.

ROSIN. I know.

JULIE. No. *(re: ROSIN's heart)* I want that. I've never felt that before. And I would like to.

MR. LEE. *(offstage)* Ms. Jackson?

ROSIN. Wait, Julie, where're you going?

JULIE. I don't know yet. I'll let you know when I find out.

    (**JULIE** *exits.*)

Epilogue

MESSICA. I finish out my junior year as fourth chair and in my senior year, I try out for mock trial – without Jessica – and find that yes, this is what I truly love. I become a lawyer and have five kids, none of them twins. And I drive them to school in a big SUV. I call my sister from time to time, and as we grow older, we come to look more and more alike. We die exactly one year apart, at the age of seventy-six and seventy-seven.

MRS. JACKSON. I get divorced. I get a second husband. And then a third. I take up the violin again. I am fantastic at it. I am fantastic at everything I do. And when my daughter goes to college, I turn her bedroom into a crafts room, like the one Martha Stewart has, and I start a blog about dogs. It becomes very, very popular. And when I go through menopause at fifty-seven, I only gain five pounds and my skin still looks amazing.

MR. LEE. I stay at San Leandro High. I never seem to get any older. I never seem to change. It seems I will become a fixture of the school until I abruptly leave my position following my arrest for trafficking apparently illegal horse tranquilizers online. Who knew!

JESSICA. I major in biology. I study diseases, how to make people sick, but I forget the part about how to make them well. I become an epidemiologist and appear on CNN discussing a recent national outbreak under my married name. This is the high point of my life.

MR. JACKSON. I get divorced. Meaning my wife divorces me. But I don't mind! We still remain friends. I move to a condo fifteen minutes from Julie and see my daughter and her family all the time. That makes me happy.

THE CUSTODIAN. The United States begins an embargo against my country. And the evil man that took over my country is overthrown and the people dance in the city square. A new president is elected and music returns to my country. I also return to my country, where I am once again a great musician and my fingers remember their love for the instrument. Or none of that happens, time goes on, and I keep cleaning up other people's messes.

REED. I have a band. It's cool. And I have a dog. And a girlfriend. And we play together. Me and my girlfriend, not the dog. I'm mostly happy till I die of a heart attack at fifty-two. It's cool. I kinda saw it coming.

ROSIN. I become first chair. And then I become a headhunter for tech companies. I find other people to do other things for other people. I am very good at my job. I am good at everything I do. And on the weekends, I teach piano to fourth graders. I never marry. I adopt a little girl from Guatamala who runs a Fortune 500 company. I never lose my love of music.

JULIE. I don't audition. I don't become first chair. I don't call Katie. Or email her. And in time, I forget that I had a friend who moved away senior year and never came back. I stay fifth chair in the orchestra, and I go to Emory for college. I like it enough. I meet a guy. I marry him. I like him enough. I have two kids: Katherine and another one whose name I always forget.

THE LOST GIRL. I stay on the island with Sven. We have children. We have grandchildren. And for the most part, I never think about music again.

Until one day, a large summer storm washes in some ocean trash and in between broken flipflops and discarded tires, I see it.

A violin.

Or a violin case.

My violin case?

I can't really tell.

But I drag it in from the shore and let it dry by the fire. And who knows what's inside or whether it'll play or whether I'll even remember how to hold my hands or what the notes are, but –

(**THE LOST GIRL** *holds up her arms, as if holding a violin.*)

Somehow in my mind, I can hear myself playing. And
it is beautiful.

> *(She begins to move her bow arm, the world's most
> beautiful music plays. The other violinists sit in
> their original chairs and make the violin gesture.
> Their violins join in. Another measure of music.)*

> *(Blackout.)*

End of Play

The Astonishing and Dangerous History of Mazefield the Frog

Jen Silverman

THE ASTONISHING AND DANGEROUS HISTORY OF MAZEFIELD THE FROG was first presented by Keen Company (Jonathan Silverstein, Artistic Director; Mark Armstrong, Director of New Work) and Samuel French, Inc. as part of the 2015 Keen Teens Festival of New Work. The performance was directed by director, with sets by Stephen H. Carmody, costumes by Katja Andreiev, lights by Rob Ross, sound by Elisheba Ittoop, and choreography by Macy Sullivan. The Production Manager was Peter Smith and the Stage manager was Sean McCain. The cast was as follows:

CLARE . . . . SaCha Coleman

SARA . . . . Olivia Hockenberry

MAZEFIELD THE FROG . . . . Yordy Rosso

THE MEANEST BOY ON THE PLANET
    / INTERNET PERSON . . . . Bahsil Moody

THE MEANEST GIRL ON THE PLANET . . . . Roza Chervinsy

FOREIGN SPY / SKATEBOARD TEEN . . . . Maya Pagan

FOREIGN SPY / SCHOOL KID . . . . Francesca Iannacone

GARFIELD THE FORMER FROG OWNER . . . . Jarek Liang

SKATEBOARD TEEN / INTERNET PERSON . . . . Juwan Wyatt

SKATEBOARD TEEN / INTERNET PERSON . . . . Steve Alvarez

CHARACTERS

CLARE – F

SARA – F

MAZEFIELD THE FROG

THE MEANEST BOY ON THE PLANET – M

THE MEANEST GIRL ON THE PLANET – F

FOREIGN SPY 1

FOREIGN SPY 2

GARFIELD THE FORMER FROG OWNER – M

SKATEBOARD TEEN 1 / INTERNET MAN 1

SKATEBOARD TEEN 2 / INTERNET MAN 2

SKATEBOARD TEEN 3 / INTERNET MAN 3

NOTES

ON CASTING & GENDER: Unless otherwise marked, characters may be played by either gender. The Internet Men can easily be played by women.

ON TEXT: The spacing is a gesture toward indicating rhythm and how thoughts change, morph, contradict each other, escalate, or get supplanted by other thoughts as we talk. The line breaks often signal either an intensification of or a shift away from something. Line breaks DO NOT indicate a beat or pause except where written.

ON MAZEFIELD: He does not wear a frog-suit, or any frog accessories. Nothing that suggests "human dressed as frog." He's just Mazefield, who happens to be a frog. He might wear jeans and chucks. If he's played by a female actor, pronouns can change.

ON SET: As minimal as possible. The pace and fluid transformation of space is more important than any props or naturalistic set pieces. Less is more.

1.

(**CLARE** *and* **SARA,** *sisters, stand over* **MAZEFIELD THE FROG.**)

CLARE. A frog?

SARA. It's for you.

CLARE. A frog.

SARA. Yay!

CLARE. Why are you giving me a frog.

SARA. It even comes with its tank.

It's a consolation prize.

CLARE. For what.

SARA. Moving here.

Being fifteen.

Being alive.

Being you.

Happy early birthday?

CLARE. Why don't *you* need a consolation prize?

SARA. Look, this boy gave it to me and I don't want it. So.

CLARE. A boy gives you things?

SARA. What.

CLARE. There are boys who give you things.

SARA. What.

CLARE. We literally *just* moved here.

SARA. I know.

CLARE. I'm stuck in study hall with The Meanest Boy On The Planet who's a mouth-breather and always sits behind me, and *you* have boys who *give* you things. Why does everything always work out for you!

SARA. I don't know.

You know. Have fun with the frog.

CLARE. I don't want a frog!

SARA. Ugh you've gotten so *difficult.*

I just can't handle you right now.

(She leaves. Beat.)

(CLARE studies MAZEFIELD.)

CLARE. Well.

You're a frog.

So.

MAZEFIELD. I never asked for this.

CLARE. What??

MAZEFIELD. It's all so overwhelmingly bleak.

CLARE. Um. What is?

MAZEFIELD. My life.

CLARE. Stop talking. You aren't supposed to talk. Stop it.

MAZEFIELD. I like talking! I like talking about the end of the world, specifically, but I'm open to other conversation topics.

CLARE. It makes me feel crazy. When you talk.

MAZEFIELD. Oh.

CLARE. I mean. I *am* crazy. But it makes me feel crazier.

MAZEFIELD. Maybe that's because you have poor listening skills.

CLARE. No, it's because I had a nervous breakdown at my old school and they moved me to this new school and my sister already has boyfriends-in-the-multiple-boyfriendzzzz and nobody even notices that I exist and now I own a frog and now it's talking to me. So.

MAZEFIELD. Oh. Well. I'm on a mission of world destruction. So.

CLARE. You're WHAT.

MAZEFIELD. Let me out of this tank and I'll explain everything.

CLARE. I can't handle this right now.

(It becomes:)

2.

(Study hall.)

(It's possible that **SKATEBOARD TEENS** *and* **MEANEST GIRL** *and* **GARFIELD** *and* **SARA** *are on stage as well. Heads down. Some are asleep.)*

(The **MEANEST BOY** *sits behind* **CLARE**.*)*

(He's definitely a mouth-breather.)

(He's also a whisper-shouter:)

MEANEST BOY. Hey!

Hey

Hey

pssst

hey

CLARE. What!

MEANEST BOY. Why don't you have any friends?

CLARE. I have friends!

MEANEST BOY. No you don't.

I never see you with them.

CLARE. Are you watching me??

MEANEST BOY. I just notice you.

So I just notice that you don't have any friends.

CLARE. I just moved here so.

I have lots of friends but they're not here.

MEANEST BOY. That's what people without friends say.

CLARE. We're not supposed to talk in study hall.

(beat)

I have a friend.

MEANEST BOY. Oh yeah who.

CLARE. You don't know him.

MEANEST BOY. Okay riiight.

CLARE. Mazefield.

MEANEST BOY. Who-field?

CLARE. His name is Mazefield.

　　He's older.

　　He could beat you up.

MEANEST BOY. Oh yeah and where is he?

CLARE. He doesn't go to school anymore.

　　He dropped out.

　　He's on a mission of world destruction.

MEANEST BOY. For real?

CLARE. He has tattoos.

　　He studies nun-chaks.

　　So. Watch out.

　　　(beat)

MEANEST BOY. Awesome.

　　　(The sound of a bell. It becomes:)

3.

(Recess.)

(SKATEBOARDS TEENS 1, 2, and 3 might do skateboard tricks. CLARE is alone. Until she is approached by The MEANEST GIRL.)

MEANEST GIRL. Hey.

CLARE. ...Um?

MEANEST GIRL. I saw you talking to my boyfriend in study hall.

CLARE. The Meanest Boy On The Planet is your boyfriend?

MEANEST GIRL. I saw you flirting.

CLARE. *He* was talking to *me.*

To be specific.

MEANEST GIRL. We're going to get married.

Keep away from him.

CLARE. Tell him to stop sitting behind me in study hall!

MEANEST GIRL. We're going to get back together, and then we're going to get married.

CLARE. You...?

MEANEST GIRL. He broke up with me because he loves me so much, it's actually physically dangerous for him, he might combust or something, like spontaneously combust from an overdose of love, so he has to keep away from me? But when the scientists get all of that under control we're going to get married, like in our senior year, or maybe by college, so. Keep away from him. Or I'll cut you.

CLARE. With what?

MEANEST GIRL. I'll find something and cut you with it. In the face.

CLARE. I'm engaged, anyway.

MEANEST GIRL. ...You are?

CLARE. Yeah.

My boyfriend is foreign, he's a foreign exchange student. He doesn't go here.

MEANEST GIRL. ...Oh.

CLARE. Yeah, he has an accent, he's a musician, he's very
exciting, he lives in a tank.

MEANEST GIRL. In a what?

CLARE. A tank. Like an army tank.

Like he's repurposed an army tank, and he lives in it.

MEANEST GIRL. Oh...

Huh...

If he's ever free

like if he's ever around

like if you're both around

we should hang out some time.

CLARE. I don't know.

MEANEST GIRL. It'll be like a double-date, we can hang out
in his tank and do homework or sniff paint-thinner or
something.

CLARE. We're busy

he writes me songs

so.

MEANEST GIRL. You should come to the school dance

it's next week

my parents are getting me a private limo

you and your boyfriend can ride in my limo

it'll be me and The Meanest Boy On The Planet

and his three friends who own skateboards (but they
promised to shower)

and we'll drink underage and take compromising selfies

and it'll be great!

CLARE. In your limo?

MEANEST GIRL. In my limo.

CLARE. Oh wow.

Uh.

I'll ask him.

MEANEST GIRL. Don't ask him, tell him.

(Everybody leaves.)

(It becomes:)

4.

(**CLARE,** *at home with* **MAZEFIELD**.)

(*She peers at him. He peers back.*)

CLARE. So. Do you still talk?

MAZEFIELD. Are you still trying to silence the voices of the oppressed?

CLARE. You still talk.

MAZEFIELD. Wanna have a nervous breakdown? Freak out? Anything?

CLARE. I have a favor to ask.

MAZEFIELD. Oh *you* have a favor! That's cute.

CLARE. I sort of maybe got myself in some trouble.

MAZEFIELD. *You're* in some trouble?

CLARE. I kind of lied. About some things.

MAZEFIELD. Okay, well, how does world destruction sound to you now?
If you're already in an ethical downward spiral?

CLARE. Not very good, frankly.

MAZEFIELD. I have post-apocalyptic fantasies but you have to have an apocalypse to have a post-apocalypse, so…

CLARE. Listen, OK
first of all I'm a pacifist
and second of all I don't like being bossed around by a homicidal vigilante frog
and third of all – WHY do you want to destroy the world?

(*beat*)

MAZEFIELD. Have you *seen* the world?

(*beat*)

CLARE. Yes.

(*beat*)

MAZEFIELD. WELL?

CLARE. I mean. Things are terrible –

MAZEFIELD. – right!

CLARE. – but you can't just destroy the world because things are terrible.

MAZEFIELD. Why not?

Let me tell you something. I'm a weird-looking frog and I was picked last at the pet store and then my owner gave me to a girl who he barely knew and then she had me for fifteen minutes before she gave me to you. And apparently nobody likes you either. So. Let's destroy the world.

(a beat)

CLARE. I'm supposed to have an older foreign musician boyfriend who lives in an army tank and can be my date to a party in a limo. And I don't have one.

MAZEFIELD. I'll find you a date.

CLARE. How?

MAZEFIELD. Online probably, that's how we order everything these days.

CLARE. I can't have an online date!!

MAZEFIELD. Why not?

CLARE. ...My mom wouldn't like it?

MAZEFIELD. The apocalypse will upset her more. It's all about comparative perspective.

CLARE. There's not going to be an apocalypse.

MAZEFIELD. Yeah there is. And if you want a date to the school dance, you're gonna help me kick it off.

CLARE. ...Like a real date?

MAZEFIELD. Oh here we go.

CLARE. Like an older, hot, tattooed, sensitive, volatile-but-not-too-volatile musician?

MAZEFIELD. Easy. Done. Shake.

CLARE. *(shakes his hand)* What am I supposed to do?

MAZEFIELD. Do you have access to any nuclear weaponry of any kind?

CLARE. What?? No!

MAZEFIELD. *(highly disappointed)* Seriously?

CLARE. I mean. I just moved here.

MAZEFIELD. Okay well, I have a KGB contact.

CLARE. Excuse me?

MAZEFIELD. And he's got a uniquely productive relationship with North Korea so.

Just prop me next to your computer.

CLARE. Are you going to broker nuclear armament deals with Russia and North Korea via my laptop?

MAZEFIELD. No, I'm gonna find you a date.

You're gonna go have coffee with emissaries from possibly Russia and possibly North Korea, but also they could have misrepresented their international affiliations for the sake of maintaining security.

CLARE. So...who are they?

MAZEFIELD. Foreign spies. That's all I know. Go meet them.

CLARE. When??

MAZEFIELD. Oh. Now, of course.

CLARE. But I don't know anything about nuclear weaponry.

MAZEFIELD. Just pretend you're my aide de camp and report back to me exactly what they say.

(It becomes:)

5.

(Split stage.)

(CLARE *in a coffee shop.* **FOREIGN SPY 1** *and* **FOREIGN SPY 2** *enter. Their faces are entirely covered with sunglasses. They might have thick fake moustaches, especially if they're women.)*

(Also: **MAZEFIELD** *online. The three* **INTERNET MEN** *stand with their backs to him. They talk without looking at him.)*

CLARE. Hi...?

MAZEFIELD. So are you *older?*

FOREIGN SPY 1. Cipher.

INTERNET MAN 1. Than what?

CLARE. What?

FOREIGN SPY 2. Beta cipher.

MAZEFIELD. I don't know, than people who aren't as old as you.

INTERNET MAN 1. I mean, yes, but isn't everyone?

MAZEFIELD. On second thought, not helpful.
Next!

CLARE. Um. Is this...? Am I...?

FOREIGN SPY 1. The guppy rises.

FOREIGN SPY 2. The minnow falls.

(They stare at **CLARE.***)*

CLARE. The...frog...is a frog?

FOREIGN SPY 2. *(with relief)* Ah! Yes.

(Both **SPIES** *sit.* **CLARE** *sits.)*

MAZEFIELD. Tattoos, yes or no?

INTERNET MAN 2. Theoretically yes!

MAZEFIELD. Theory isn't helpful, tattoos are. So: yes / no?

INTERNET MAN 2. I've been thinking about getting a small tasteful one.

MAZEFIELD. Taste isn't in demand here. Next!

FOREIGN SPY 1. The sun rises.

FOREIGN SPY 2. The moon sets.

(They stare at **CLARE.***)*

CLARE. ...Sometimes it rains?

FOREIGN SPY 1. Ah yes.

FOREIGN SPY 2. Yes yes.

MAZEFIELD. Musician, yes or no?

INTERNET MAN 3. I have a band.

MAZEFIELD. What's it called?

INTERNET MAN 3. The Freudian Thrashings.

FOREIGN SPY 2. Alpacas.

FOREIGN SPY 1. Al Capone.

CLARE. ...Apocalypse!

(The **SPIES** *suddenly confer together, very seriously.)*

...What did I say?

MAZEFIELD. Very promising.

How volatile are you?

INTERNET MAN 3. My therapist and my wife both think
I'm fairly volatile.

MAZEFIELD. Oh. Your wife?

INTERNET MAN 3. What?

MAZEFIELD. This isn't working.

INTERNET MAN 1. What isn't?

MAZEFIELD. The internet.

Twenty-first century relationships.

Procuring a prom date for my friend.

Thanks anyway.

(The **SPIES** *return to face* **CLARE.***)*

(very somber)

FOREIGN SPY 1. The snow falls.

FOREIGN SPY 2. The cedars bend.

CLARE. Hang on...

FOREIGN SPY 1. See you at the school dance, Mazefield.

CLARE. I'm not Mazefield!

FOREIGN SPY 2. That's what he told us he'd say.

(They leave.)

(It becomes:)

6.

(Study hall.)

(The **MEANEST GIRL** *sits behind* **CLARE***.)*

(The **MEANEST BOY** *sits behind her.)*

MEANEST GIRL. Hey!
Hey
pssst
hey

CLARE. What!

MEANEST GIRL. So what do you think about my limo
and bringing your hot older boyfriend
and maybe he can use his ID to get us vodka
and we can take shots in the limo like a bad movie
about Bad Teens Who Do Bad Things
and it'll be fun and we'll be friends.

CLARE. I don't know yet.

MEANEST GIRL. What is there to not know?

MEANEST BOY. Pssssst hey are you talking about a party am
I invited?

CLARE. I asked my hot older boyfriend and he said he
didn't know.

MEANEST GIRL. Text him, text him right now.

MEANEST BOY. Pssst hey I wanna come, I heard your
boyfriend owns a tank.

CLARE. I forgot my cell, I forgot it at home.

MEANEST GIRL. Nobody forgets their phone, I sleep with
my phone in my hand, like glued to my hand, like
literally once I super-glued it to my hand, text your hot
older boyfriend!

MEANEST BOY. I heard he's a sniper, like in the army, like
in the special forces, like he's a Navy Seal?

CLARE. He doesn't text, he doesn't check his phone that
much, I'll ask him after school.

(Faster and faster:)

MEANEST GIRL. Tell him to bring vokda

MEANEST BOY. – or hand grenades –

MEANEST GIRL. – you're not invited –

MEANEST BOY. – or a necklace made of human teeth –

MEANEST GIRL. – you broke up with me you broke my heart –

MEANEST BOY. – I'm not talking to you I'm talking to her –

MEANEST GIRL. – well she's my friend, she hates you too –

MEANEST BOY. – she's MY friend –

MEANEST GIRL. She is NOT your friend, she's MY friend.

MEANEST BOY. YOU'RE SO CRAZY, WE NEVER EVEN DATED.

(A shocked silence. Everybody looks at them.)

CLARE. May I be excused?

(She leaves. It becomes:)

7.

(**CLARE** *and* **MAZEFIELD**, *at home.*)

CLARE. I mean, NOBODY? You didn't find ANYBODY?

MAZEFIELD. Nobody fit your specifications. Can we talk about the foreign spies?

CLARE. This is terrible. I'm never going to have any friends or go to school dances or live the sort of lifestyle that bad teens live in bad movies where they do bad things and have so much more fun than I'm having right now.

MAZEFIELD. How were the spies?

CLARE. I didn't really understand anything they said?

MAZEFIELD. Are you being racist or sexist or xenophobic?

CLARE. I don't think so? We talked about weather patterns –

MAZEFIELD. – yes yes, very good –

CLARE. And then we talked about the apocalypse.

MAZEFIELD. Oh!!

CLARE. And then one of them said, "See you at the school dance."

MAZEFIELD. Oh.

CLARE. And they called me Mazefield.

     – Is that a good-Oh or a bad-Oh?

MAZEFIELD. It means the plan is going forward sooner than expected.

CLARE. Okay!

     So.

     Here's the thing.

     World destruction or not,

     I might

     just

     have

     to go

     to prom

     with YOU.

MAZEFIELD. ...Me?

CLARE. You.

MAZEFIELD. ...With you?

CLARE. With me.

MAZEFIELD. No!

CLARE. Well, I'm about to lose all the friends I sort of didn't have.

And then I'll be ugly and sad and alone while being surrounded by fun cool people.

And then, it sounds like the world is going to end?

So you might as well keep me company. You're pretty good company.

You can wear a bow-tie.

MAZEFIELD. I don't dance.

CLARE. You hop.

MAZEFIELD. I hop but I don't dance.

CLARE. We can just sort of stand on the sidelines.

MAZEFIELD. I don't drink.

CLARE. I mean, I'm underage.

MAZEFIELD. I don't want to make out with you.

CLARE. We don't have to make out.

> *(beat – insulted)*

...Why not?

MAZEFIELD. ...Did you want to?

CLARE. I mean I don't want to make out so I'm not saying I want to make out, but just, why DON'T you want to make out?

MAZEFIELD. Don't take it personally, I just wouldn't feel comfortable.

CLARE. Oh.

MAZEFIELD. And also, I'm a frog.

CLARE. Well I *know* you're a frog.

MAZEFIELD. Okay.

CLARE. I didn't want to make out with you, that wasn't what I was saying, anyway.

>   *(beat)*

Look, if the world is gonna end, you might as well get out and have some fun. I don't think there's any fun, in the post-apocalypse.

>   *(beat)*

MAZEFIELD. You said a bow-tie?

CLARE. Is that a deal-breaker?

MAZEFIELD. I could wear a bow-tie.

CLARE. Okay.

>   *(It becomes:)*

8.

(The school dance!)

(Everybody is there, milling, awkward. As awkward as possible.)

(Ad-lib a low hum of awkward conversation, nothing too distinguishable, but people talking to each other, or avoiding talking to each other. Music plays. School dance type music.)

(Enter: **CLARE** *and* **MAZEFIELD**.*)*

(He's wearing a bow-tie. He looks pretty good.)

CLARE. Let's just stand at the back wall for twenty minutes, and then we can go.

MAZEFIELD. You got dressed up to be here for twenty minutes?

CLARE. I mean I had to come so that I wouldn't be the girl who misses the school dance, but actually it's gonna suck so we should probably just go.

MAZEFIELD. Not until the world ends.

(As they stand against the wall...)

MEANEST BOY. Hey it's Clare.

MEANEST GIRL. Whatever.

SKATEBOARD TEEN 1. Who?

SKATEBOARD TEEN 2. Where?

SKATEBOARD TEEN 3. What's a Clare?

MEANEST BOY. She's in my study hall. She sits in front of me.

MEANEST GIRL. She's weird.

SKATEBOARD TEEN 1. Never heard of her.

SKATEBOARD TEEN 2. Never noticed her.

SKATEBOARD TEEN 3. Don't care. But her friend looks...

SKATEBOARD TEEN 1. Weird.

SKATEBOARD TEEN 2. Scary?

SKATEBOARD TEEN 3. Awesome.

MEANEST GIRL. Dreamy.

MEANEST BOY. ...Dreamy?

MEANEST GIRL. Foreign.

Not like anybody I know.

Not like anybody I've ever seen.

MEANEST BOY. He looks kind of like a frog...?

MEANEST GIRL. Exotic.

I'm going to go talk to him.

(She goes over to **CLARE** *and* **MAZEFIELD**.*)*

HI.

CLARE. Oh! Uh! Hi!

MEANEST GIRL. Is this your boyfriend?

CLARE. This? Uh –

MEANEST GIRL. You look like you're not from here!

MAZEFIELD. Oh. I'm not.

MEANEST GIRL. Awesome! Where are you from? Are there beaches? Are there mandolins? Do you have an accent?

MAZEFIELD. Um...

*(***SARA** *enters, with her date,* **GARFIELD**.*)*

SARA. Oh it's my sister.

GARFIELD. You have a sister?

SARA. Yeah I didn't mention her before because she's a loser and she smells weird and she doesn't talk to human beings and I was sort of hoping you'd never meet her? But anyway there she is.

GARFIELD. What's she doing with my frog?

SARA. *(blinks)* Oh!

Is that...?

Wow, he's...grown.

GARFIELD. Has she been overfeeding him? Maybe she overfed him.

SARA. Is he wearing a...bow-tie?

GARFIELD. I'm just really confused about why you'd give your sister my frog, when I gave him to you, because you're really pretty and I wanted to give you something meaningful, but then you gave it to your sister, which is sort of like throwing it away? – and also I didn't even know you had a sister.

SARA. I mean. I don't like frogs.

GARFIELD. Oh.

SARA. You could have given me flowers?

GARFIELD. I didn't have flowers.

SARA. Okay well, if you'd given me flowers, I wouldn't have given them to my sister.

CLARE. Hey Sara.

SARA. *(pretending not to see her, until she can't anymore)* Who? What? Where? ...Oh hi.

MAZEFIELD. Hey Garfield.

GARFIELD. You talk?

MAZEFIELD. Yeah.

GARFIELD. I never knew that.

MAZEFIELD. I never talked to you.

GARFIELD. How come??

MAZEFIELD. You didn't seem that intelligent.

GARFIELD. Oh.

MAZEFIELD. And I was on a mission of world destruction and I was looking for an accomplice and I couldn't really afford anybody second-rate, you know?

SARA. *(to CLARE)* Is that my dress? That looks like my dress.

CLARE. You weren't wearing it.

SARA. Oh my god what have I said about touching my things.

Oh also your frog is talking.

CLARE. Yeah he talks.

SARA. Weird.

Can you *not* borrow my shit without asking?

CLARE. You weren't around to ask.

GARFIELD. Wait…did you call me second-rate?

I'm not second-rate.

MAZEFIELD. Don't take it personally, it's just an observation.

MEANEST GIRL. Oh my GOD, are those your hot foreign FRIENDS?

> *(Everybody turns and looks.)*

> *(The* **FOREIGN SPIES** *have entered. They're trying to be unobtrusive but actually they're extremely noticeable. The Mardi Gras beads and gigantic sunglasses don't help.)*

CLARE. Oh!

SARA. Whoa.

GARFIELD. I'm actually really smart for my age.

MEANEST GIRL. This is such a great party!!!

School dances are usually so lame!!!

Intro me to your friends immediately!

FOREIGN SPY 1. I am American Teen.

FOREIGN SPY 2. Nothing happening here!

FOREIGN SPY 1. No need to look!

FOREIGN SPY 2. Just normal.

FOREIGN SPY 1. How's your homework?

FOREIGN SPY 2. I have so much homework!

FOREIGN SPY 1. Me too!

> *(They beam at each other. Just normal American teens!)*

MAZEFIELD. *(urgently)* The snow falls.

FOREIGN SPY 1. *(caught up in the fantasy)* I like to watch YouTube!

MAZEFIELD. *(increasing urgency)* The rain rains!

FOREIGN SPY 2. *(also caught up)* I like the String Cheese.

MAZEFIELD. Snow Falling On Cedars!!

FOREIGN SPY 1. I text you with my iDevice.

FOREIGN SPY 2. I text you back!

FOREIGN SPY 1. I send emoticons.

FOREIGN SPY 2. I take selfie!

FOREIGN SPY 1. I take selfie too!!

(*They beam at each other, even more delighted.*)

MAZEFIELD. (*losing it*) Do you have the nuclear weapons with you or not?!

(*a beat*)

(*Everybody looks at him.*)

CLARE. Uh...

SKATEBOARD TEEN 1. Did he say...?

SKATEBOARD TEEN 2. Nuclear...

SKATEBOARD TEEN 3. Weapons???

MEANEST GIRL. Whoa.

MEANEST BOY. Awesome!

SARA. Yikes.

GARFIELD. I'm actually really smart.

(*beat*)

FOREIGN SPY 1. (*to* **CLARE**) Ah... Mazefield, yes?

CLARE. No, he's Mazefield.

FOREIGN SPY 2. He told us he'd say that.

MAZEFIELD. Where is your apocalypse-achieving nuclear weaponry??

FOREIGN SPY 2. You are, as we say, "blowing our cover."

MAZEFIELD. I don't care about your cover! Let's blow up the world!

CLARE. I'm really not Mazefield.

FOREIGN SPY 1. (*uncomfortable*) Ah...you see...

FOREIGN SPY 2. How do we say this...

FOREIGN SPY 1. It is too late.

MAZEFIELD. Too late??
How is it too late?

FOREIGN SPY 2. Well...

FOREIGN SPY 1. Look around you.

FOREIGN SPY 2. The world? Is already destroyed.

MAZEFIELD. What? No it isn't!

FOREIGN SPY 1. The rainforests?

FOREIGN SPY 2. The baby seals?

FOREIGN SPY 1. The ozone layer?

FOREIGN SPY 2. The "strip-malls"?

FOREIGN SPY 1. The "youth culture"?

FOREIGN SPY 2. Ugh.

FOREIGN SPY 1. Too late.

FOREIGN SPY 2. Bye bye world.

FOREIGN SPY 1. At least there is YouTube.

MAZEFIELD. But – ! But!

FOREIGN SPY 2. At least there is String Cheese.

GARFIELD. (I like string cheese.)

FOREIGN SPY 1. At least there is American Teen School Dance.

FOREIGN SPY 1. I have never before been to American Teen School Dance!

FOREIGN SPY 2. Let's dance!

> *(They begin a dance party.)*

> *(Eventually everybody dances.)*

> *(**MAZEFIELD** and **CLARE** stand to the side.)*

> *(**MAZEFIELD** is in a state of shock.)*

CLARE. Are you OK?

I'm sorry about all of this.

I mean I'm glad they didn't blow up the world, but...

Are you sure you're OK?

MAZEFIELD. *(dawning delight)* We're *already* in the post-apocalypse.

CLARE. Uh...

MAZEFIELD. He just told me the word has finally ended. Possibly while we were in here!

CLARE. I mean he didn't quite – ?

MAZEFIELD. I could be leading a zombie army right now.

CLARE. I mean, the ozone layer is a real problem...but he didn't exactly...*zombies* aren't quite...?

MEANEST BOY. Did you say zombies?

MAZEFIELD. They're a problem.

MEANEST BOY. They're a real problem!

MAZEFIELD. Abort Mission: World Destruction.
Commence Mission: Zombie Army.

MEANEST BOY. Can I come, and we can hang out in your tank?

MAZEFIELD. Um...you wanna hang out in my tank?

MEANEST BOY. Yeah man, I can't believe you own a tank.

MAZEFIELD. Okay, well, let's go.

      (to **CLARE***)*

You coming?

FOREIGN SPY 1. Clare! Come do American Teen Dance with us!

FOREIGN SPY 2. Yes, show us how Real American Teen does American Teen Moves!

MEANEST GIRL. Oh my god I'll totally show you.

FOREIGN SPY 1. Clare!

CLARE. I'll be home soon.

MAZEFIELD. Cool. See you at the end of the world.

CLARE. See you there.

      (She joins the dance party.)

      (Dancing! The **SPIES** *do crazy moves.)*

      (It's awesome.)

      (blackout)

End of Play